The Consolations

The Consolations

Poems by

J.R. Solonche

© 2025 J.R. Solonche. All rights reserved.
This material may not be reproduced in any form, published,
reprinted, recorded, performed, broadcast,
rewritten or redistributed without
the explicit permission of J.R. Solonche.
All such actions are strictly prohibited by law.

Cover design by Shay Culligan
Cover image by *The Cult of Venus* by Magnus Enckell, 1895,
the Finnish National Gallery via Europeana on Unsplash
Author photo by Emily Solonche

ISBN: 978-1-63980-857-1

Kelsay Books
502 South 1040 East, A-119
American Fork, Utah 84003
Kelsaybooks.com

Books by J.R. Solonche

Criticism

An Aesthetic Toward Notes: On Poets & Poetry

Poems

Alone
The Architect's House
Around Here
Barren Road
Beautiful Day
The Black Birch
The Book of a Small Fisherman
Collected Short Poems
Coming To
The Dreams of the Gods
The Dust
The Eglantine
Enjoy Yourself
The Five Notebooks of Zhao Li
For All I Know
God
A Guide of the Perplexed
Heart's Content
I, Emily Dickinson & Other Found Poems
If You Should See Me Walking on the Road
In a Public Place
In Short Order

Invisible
The Jewish Dancing Master
Leda
Life-Size
The Lost Notebook of Zhao Li
The Moon Is the Capital of the World
Night Visit
Old
Peach Girl: Poems for a Chinese Daughter (with Joan I. Siegel)
Piano Music
The Porch Poems
Reading Takuboku Ishikawa
Selected Poems 2002–2021
Then Morning
The Time of Your Life
Tomorrow, Today, and Yesterday
To Say the Least
True Enough
Won't Be Long
Years Later

Contents

Elegy for Richard Serra	13
There Was a Cloud	14
Two Flags	15
Or Not	16
Zhao Li Notices	17
What If	18
Alpha & Omega	19
Zhao Li Stops	20
Zhao Li Goes Outside	21
Again Zhao Li	22
Woken Up by the Sun	23
Dead Snake on the Road	24
Apologetics	25
September	26
A Cloud	27
Every Day	28
Patience	29
Early Autumn Pastoral	30
To a Spider	31
Now	32
Zhao Li Remembers	33
Zhao Li Cannot	34
Sometimes Zhao Li	35
Red Wine	36
The Sky	37
You Said the Reading	38
I Was Going to Say	39
Love Song	40
Zhao Li Pauses	41
Happiness	42
Crickets	43

Stranded	44
The Good Word	45
Movie	46
O Lady	47
Zhao Li Has	48
Late September Pastoral	49
Zhao Li Sits	50
Tuesday Poem	51
Yesterday	52
Chinese Poems	53
The Bronx	54
Haircut	55
Zhao Li Looks Up	56
October	57
Birdbath	58
My Father	59
Four A.M.	60
Fall	62
Short October Pastoral	63
Habitual Dream	64
Yellow Chrysanthemums	65
I Cannot Sleep	66
Dusk	67
Three Petunias	68
The Wild Black Cherry	69
This Morning	70
The Joy of Loneliness	71
This Morning	72
View of a Lake	73
Baseball	74
Tree Stump and Boulder	75

Tree in Late October	76
Rachel	77
A Reading	78
Short Late October Pastoral	79
Dream	80
First Day with Feeder	81
The Library	82
Zhao Li Pauses	83
Three Deer	84
Zhao Li Finishes the Poem He Began 70 Years Ago	85
Dreams	86
Irony	87
Shangri-La	88
November Woods	89
Two Dogs	90
Youth	91
Prayer	92
War	93
Empty Field in Which There Used to Be Three Horses	94
Zhao Li Wanted to Know	95
Songbird in the Snow	96
Snow	97
The Consolations	98

Elegy for Richard Serra

(November 2, 1938–March 26, 2024)

Which of the Serras will be his?
Which Serra will be Richard Serra's?
Of his steel walls, which will be his own
steel wall, his own steel stone,
his own steel memorial?
No, you cannot say that all
of them will be. Only one can suit
him, one only rusted armor fit
to keep him safe and sound
against the cold breath
of the dragon Time, going around
and around and around with Death.
So which of the Serras is his?
Which Serra is Richard Serra's?

There Was a Cloud

There was a cloud
just now. I swear
I saw a cloud in the
corner of the sky
out of the corner of
my eye just now, or
I would not have
believed this blue
thing above me—is
it an inverted bowl?
is it a sea? is it a mural
of a deserted heaven?
is it a dream? is it real
at all?—were the sky.

Two Flags

A truck with two flags
flying from the bed, an
American flag—all right—
and a candidate's flag—
bad flag from a bad man—
why not the swastika?
It's what you really want,
isn't it? But that would
be too much, even for you,
even for such a one as you,
my townsman, my neighbor,
my fellow citizen of America.

Or Not

Unlike you, Bill, I
do not dance naked
(or not) in my room,
north (or not), singing
(or not), but nevertheless,
like you, I am lonely,
born so (or not), I am
lonely, best so (or not),
happy (or not), at home
(or not) or not.

Zhao Li Notices

a hummingbird circling around the feeder,
but it is not alighting on the perch
to feed. "Ah, I know what you are saying,
Brother Hummingbird, for that is what
I do when my wine cupboard is empty,"
laughs Zhao Li as he goes in to prepare
the sugar water to fill the feeder.

What If

I have thought this often.
What if I am thinking of you
at the very moment you are
thinking of me? I know there
is no way of knowing now, yet
somehow, I think we would
know, don't you think?

Alpha & Omega

The last does not know
anymore it is the last
than the first knows it
is the first, but of course,
I might be wrong on both counts.

Zhao Li Stops

to listen to the crickets.
Or are they tree frogs?
"What does it matter if Zhao
Li knows which he listens
to, crickets or tree frogs?
What matters is that the
crickets and the tree frogs
know," Zhao Li laughs.

Zhao Li Goes Outside

to write but has forgotten
to bring paper. "Just as well.
I have also forgotten to bring
a poem," he laughs.

Again Zhao Li

goes outside to write,
and this time he remembers
to bring paper but now has
forgotten a pen. "Just as well.
I have also neglected the poem
I wanted to write yesterday,"
smiles Zhao Li without laughing.

Woken Up by the Sun

at his window, Zhao Li
curses it for interrupting
his beautiful dream. Then
he hears the singing of the
first bird of the morning.
"Oh, are you also cursing
the sun for waking you from
your dream?" he asks. "No,
Zhao Li, I am blessing the sun.
But what is a dream?" says
the bird. "Well, since you
bless the sun for awakening
you, you are lucky, for you need
not know of dreams," sighs Zhao Li.

Dead Snake on the Road

It was about timing.
This young snake, no
more than eight inches
long but hard to tell since
it was omega-shaped,
just there, just then, for its
rendezvous with the tire,
not a moment too soon,
not a moment too late.
It was about timing.
As always. As everywhere.

Apologetics

Not a day goes by without
an apology from me. I will
apologize for something I did
or did not do or for something
I said or did not say. If I am out
in public, I will apologize to
strangers for not looking where
I'm going. At home, I apologize
to friends who call me for not
calling them, or to the spider
for carelessly sweeping away
its web, or to all the poems I send
out into the world unprepared—
Oh my children!—my apologies.

September

School begins, and how
differently it begins for them,
for the five-year olds waiting
with mothers, or with fathers
sometimes, for the first day
of the first week of the first year,
excited, brave, they board the bus
as golden as a sunrise, while for
the teenagers, singly or in pairs,
already they look defeated, worn
down, morose, resentful, old,
"We are old," they think as they get on
this sunset bus of their own.

A Cloud

But which cloud?
Shall it be this one
directly overhead
for which I must
incline my head all
the way back to see?
Yes, it is worth it,
the whitest one,
a crab's ghost,
or shall it be that one
just now arriving
from the east, a thing
of string, of wisps
swiped by the wind,
bread crumbs for the birds,
or shall it be neither, but
rather the one gray as
a battleship, the one
that darkens the day for
three minutes, the one
that swallows the shadows?
Yes, this cloud, the one
that shadows the sun.

Every Day

Every day as I go out
I think of you, Bill, and how
you wished "that Aristotle
had gone on
to a consideration of the dithyrambic
poem—or that his notes had survived,"
and I wish I could think
of something to wish myself,
but I am selfish, even narcissistic,
and all I can wish is to have a flower
named for me, or a tree,
or best of all, a stream so clear,
so like a mirror,
the homely may see themselves
transformed therein.
Perhaps if there were a garden
to walk through it would be different,
but there isn't a garden.
There is only a road going around
and around.

Patience

I tell the hummingbird to be patient.
The sugar water is cooling in the kitchen.
I will bring it out soon.
Soon the red glass feeder will be full again.
Is there no one to tell me to be patient other than myself?
How many times do I tell myself to be patient but to no avail?

Early Autumn Pastoral

Let's call it fall.
Yes, let's.
Autumn belongs to Keats.
As do *melancholy* and *urn* and *thrall*.

To a Spider

How quickly you built it back,
the web I tore from its moorings
when I got up from my chair
and went the wrong way taking
the silken supports with me
on my neck and shoulders.
Oh elegant engineer. Oh brilliant
builder. You have my word as
a lover of webs, I will remember
which way to go.

Now

Now is not the time for the trivial,
for the frivolous.
Now is the time to dust off the old books,
the tomes with the pages yellow
as the desert sands,
with the words solid as the granite of ancient tombs.
Do you see it?
The world now is different and the same.
Do you see it?
The world is the same and different, utterly different now.

Zhao Li Remembers

that he was young once.
He wipes a tear from his eye.
Then he remembers that now he is old
and wipes another tear from his eye.
"Why there is no third tear? Is it because
 I have nothing more to remember?" he sighs.

Zhao Li Cannot

get enough of the hummingbirds
even if those who read
his poems complain that he
gives them too much.
But it is September, and the days
are shorter, and the air is cooler,
and the hummingbirds will soon
be gone, but those who read
Zhao Li's poems will still complain
about the hummingbirds that are gone.

Sometimes Zhao Li

thinks he knows what
consciousness is, and
sometimes he does not
think he knows what
consciousness is.

Red Wine

Yes, it is blood.
Who am I to say it is not?
So yes, it is blood but not the blood of any god.
It is the blood of music, and poetry is its body.

The Sky

This afternoon the sky has
more blue than it knows
what to do with. "Give us
some blue," say the trees,
"for we are tired of always
being green." "Give us some
blue," say the grasses, "for we,
too, are tired of always being
green." "Give me some blue,"
says the hummingbird, "for I
am tired of always being ruby-
throated." "Give us some
blue," say the marigolds, "for
we are tired of always being
yellow." "No," says the smug
sky, "for if I give you all some
of my blue, how will the world
know where to find heaven?"

You Said the Reading

You said the reading
was "Extraordinary,"
and I am glad that it was,
but I'm surprised because
I've read the poems he read,
and they are ordinary, just
ordinary poems lying there
on the page, supine, eyes
closed, breathing through
the mouth, barely awake,
too weak to sit up straight.

I Was Going to Say

that if I were these marigolds
now, I would not know how
I would feel about that
hummingbird that zipped
by with barely a glance
my way, but I do know, for
I would feel what I felt in
high school when Deirdre
Herrick zipped by in the hall
way with barely a glance my way.

Love Song

Of whom do I lie
here thinking? Of
so many, so many,
and of none. Such is
my mysterious math,
my miserable equation.
But it is no mystery, for
I am laying it all out
lying here.

Zhao Li Pauses

to address the sun struggling
to shine through the morning haze.
"Oh, there you are, Old Soul Old
Sol, so now you know how old Zhao
Li feels when he struggles to shine
through morning haze after not
getting a good night's sleep," he laughs.

Happiness

They do look happier now
that the petunias are gone,
half drowned in all the rain,
the remainder eaten by
the deer, the marigolds nodding
in approval in the breeze.

Crickets

In the weedy grass, the crickets
chirp a signal I have never learned.
It could be about the weather later
today or about the kind of winter
we're in for, or it may say nothing useful
for anyone but themselves: "I am here,
sweetie, over here in the weedy grass
behind you. Please come before it's too
late." Yet this, too, could signal the kind
of winter we're all in for.

Stranded

Don't you envy them,
this man and this woman,
alone up there, waiting for
their ride home so weightlessly?

The Good Word

"What's the good word?"
asked the postmaster as
I came into the post office.
"Fuckemall," I said. "Is that
good enough?" I was in a bad
mood. "Yeah, not bad, but
I've got a better one," he said.
"What is it" I said. "Scroom,"
he said. "Scroom? How do
you spell that?" I said. He wrote
it down for me—S C R O O M.
"Oh, *screw him,*" I said. "Or
screw them," he said. "You're
right. That is a better word than
mine," I said as I was leaving
with my mail. "And don't forget.
I invented it," he said. "You sure
it doesn't already exist?" I said.
"No fucking way," he said. When
I got home, I looked it up. It does
exist. It's in the *Urban Dictionary.*
It means "the disembodied
spirit of an owl. Also known as
Scroomsaw, in which case the soul
has not left the owl." I'm not going
to tell him. No fucking way.

Movie

It was long.
Probably too long.
Not the sort of movie
you would want to see
more than once.
It was based on true events.
Not the sort of true events
you would want to happen
more than once.

O Lady

Blame your beauty, yes,
your lips, your eyes, your hair
are to blame for my stare,
but do not deny
that I lingered there
because of what I saw
with my better eyes, the better part
that was beauty's beating heart.

Zhao Li Has

a shot of whiskey.
He feels good but
not good enough,
so he has another shot.
He feels better but
still not good enough,
so he has a third shot.
"Ah, now I feel good
enough," mumbles
Zhao Li as he dozes off.

Late September Pastoral

How reluctant is green to go.
You can hear it—Listen—say, "No, no, no."

I haven't seen the hummingbirds in days.
I never had the chance to bid them, "Adios."

The garden has been taken by small white flowers.
Are they preparing us for the snow of winter?

Yet here is a small white butterfly.
It is the ghost of a green dragonfly.

And here comes the call of a crow.
And there goes the call of a crow.

Zhao Li Sits

on a rock by the side
of the road. Or is it a stone?
Zhao Li calls it a "rock" when
he wants to write a poem
with words that rhyme with
"rock." He calls it a "stone"
when he wants to write a
poem with words that rhyme
with "stone." But today Zhao
Li's back is very painful, too
painful for him to contemplate
writing either poem, so he
just sits down to ease his back.
"Ah, that line rhymes with both
stone and *rock*," he laughs.

Tuesday Poem

It is good to be in the sun,
so, so good, there is nothing
better to be in in October
when the sun wears its Sunday
best, even on a Tuesday, which
I believe is today although
nothing announces it, not
the crows, not the hawks, not
the last of the dragonflies,
who know no more than I know.
Why should they, why should they
know more than how good, how
so, so good it is to be in the sun?

Yesterday

We're not done yet
with each other,
yesterday and I, for
there is one thing
more to forget.

Chinese Poems

I love looking at Chinese poems.
I love looking at Chinese poems more
than at any other poems.
I cannot read Chinese, so I have to say
that I look at them.
I love them because they are beautiful to look at
and since they all look the same to me,
they are all beautiful.
That they do not mean the same doesn't matter at all,
for they are all beautiful the same way,
like a strange and wonderful world inhabited only by
chrysanthemums.

The Bronx

I met a man from The Bronx.
He was from the south Bronx, not my part,
the north Bronx, the uptown Bronx.
But we understood each other perfectly.
O Bronx!

Haircut

I watch her work in the mirror,
Julie from Slovenia.
How deft she is with scissors and fingers,
and then how artful with blow dryer and brush.
The other one comes with the broom to sweep the hair,
all the hair that has fallen in cascades from my head to the floor.
I wonder what will happen to it.
I do not ask.
"All done, you're all beautified," she says.
And so I am, so I am.
All beautified and lightified,
I walk out into brightness,
all the beatitude of all the afternoon light
brightified uponified all of me.

Zhao Li Looks Up

at the clear blue sky.
"Would I were as clear and as blue
as you are," he says to the sky.
"And so shall you be, Zhao Li,
and so shall you be," says the sky
in its most serious voice.

October

A breath of wind
between the shafts
of sun. It is cool, which
the sun already is too
weak to warm. The world
is changing around me.
I, too, am changing as
my patience grows cooler.

Birdbath

The top, the bath, is
missing. Now only
the tripod stands
between the garden
and the weedy grass
at the wood's edge.
The other day,
I chanced to see a crow
land on it, look me in the eye,
and tell me my fortune
in one quick *caw* before flying off.

My Father

Unlike the fathers of my friends,
my father was no athlete,
but he shot a mean game of pool,
he had a 185 bowling average,
and when he was in the mood,
he would show me the broken knuckle
he got playing softball.
This is all I remember,
and even if I could remember more,
this is all he would want said anyway.

Four A.M.

I am awake.
It is dark.
There is light at the window.
As I walk to the stairs, I pause to look.

It is stars.
It is galaxies.
It is universes.

The stars say, "Do not worry.
We are not going anywhere.
We'll be here when you are ready, for we've been waiting for you
    all our lives."

The galaxies say, "Do not worry.
We are not going anywhere.
We'll be here when you are ready, for we've been waiting for you
    all our lives."

The universes say, "Do not worry.
We are not going anywhere.
We'll be here when you are ready, for we've been waiting for you
    all our lives."

I go downstairs to the bathroom.
When I come upstairs, I look out the window.

There are the stars that have been waiting for me all their lives.
There are the galaxies that have been waiting for me all their lives.
There are the universes that have been waiting for me all their
    lives.

I do not worry.
I fall asleep.
I dream of what it means to be ready.

Fall

The leaves, yellow now
and anxious, make
the wind work. "Try harder,"
they tease. "You can do better
than that," they taunt.
And it does.
The wind does do better than that.

Short October Pastoral

The day awakens to cold rain.
The night says, "It's all yours," and goes back to sleep.

The sky is carrying a golden umbrella.
The last of the marigolds struggle to keep their heads up.

"Put us out of our misery," they say.
"Do not let us die of the cold as the petunias did."

"Soon," I tell them. "Soon."
"I am their witness," calls a crow.

Habitual Dream

It should be nonsense
to call a dream a habit,
but I call it that, a bad
habit, like smoking,
which I broke after many
attempts, or loudly talking
over someone, which I am
slowly but surely breaking,
this habitual dream that
begins differently each time
but that ends always the same,
this dream that is stronger
than nicotine, that is stronger
than the ego of my voice.

Yellow Chrysanthemums

It should be the only
color allowed, this
bright sunlight yellow
for this afternoon
yellow sunlight on
all the porches in town.

I Cannot Sleep

I cannot sleep.
I go out.
I do not have to look up to see
that the stars fill every corner of the night.
The stars overwhelm me.
Homesickness overwhelms me.
"You must go back to where you came from," they say.
"Yes, yes," I say. "I must go back."
But for which one, for which one am I homesick?

Dusk

On an ocean
of shadows,
the sun furls
its golden sail
but, nevertheless,
still follows
the wind west.

Three Petunias

If this were yours, Alfred,
it would be a metaphor.
Like the "Three Roses," that
one that wasn't about three
flowers, but this is mine,
and it's no metaphor. It
really is a poem about three
flowers, the last petunias
standing in the pot by
the front door in October.
Don't get me wrong. I'm
not equating them. Yours
is so much better. They
always are, the flowers
and the metaphors.

The Wild Black Cherry

in October is half
a year from April
when it will be born
again, but the leaves,
yellow and forlorn, do
not know it, for they
cannot hear the roots
whispering to them
from deep in the earth,
"Soon, soon, soon."

This Morning

At 7:15 this morning,
a crow calls ridicule
on the sky as it tries
on the full moon, which
is two sizes too small.

The Joy of Loneliness

I was lonely.
I looked in the mirror
and knew the joy
of another's loneliness.
It was the loneliness of our joy.

This Morning

something moved in the trees.
It did not have wings, so it wasn't a bird.
It did not speak, so it wasn't the wind.
It did not darken the leaves, so it was not a shadow.
It was nothing.
Nothing moved in the trees.
What moved in the trees was nothing.

View of a Lake

Unobstructed save for
a split rail fence, more
invitation than obstruction,
and a swing set with slide
on which there are no
children, mysteriously,
on this sunny Sunday,
the lake spreads out in
a miracle of emptiness.

Baseball

My favorite baseball poem
is "At the Ball Game" by
William Carlos Williams.
It's my favorite because it
isn't really about baseball
at all but about the crowd,
which "is moved uniformly
by a spirit of uselessness
which delights them . . ." In
other words, it's about
the human condition. No,
it's not what you think, not
a metaphor for the human
condition. "The flashy female
with her/ mother, gets it . . ."
and "the Jew gets it straight . . ."
Listen to the "cheering,
the crowd is laughing/ in detail/
permanently, seriously
without thought," says Williams.
Without thought. That's the key.

Tree Stump and Boulder

How much older
this boulder is
than the oak tree
stump next to it,
yet how much older
the stump looks, a darker,
deeper, more shriveled
old, a more wrinkled
and grayer old, a meaner,
much more angry old.

Tree in Late October

I do not know what it is
other than ugly, which
is just as well, not wishing
to insult it by name and not
just because it is fall and
its leaves are gone, leaving
it naked, exposed before
the world, while at least
in summer they do it
the kindness of a shape.

Rachel

You are a coward.
You should have been there.
You should have held me.
You should have been the one I saw.
Yours should have been the last face.
Yours should have been the last eyes.
Your eyes should have been in my eyes.
Your heart should have been with my heart.
Your breath should have been with my breath.
You were not there.
You are a coward.
I will not forgive you.
I will come in your dreams.
I am there now.
I will draw blood.
I am now.
But at least you have done this.
This thing.
The thing that is the most you can do.
That you can ever do.
I don't understand this thing.
I never did.
You are a coward.

A Reading

In the middle of a poem,
a woman yawned. He stopped
and asked if he was boring her.
She said he was. He sighed. He
smiled and said he was boring
himself. Then he read the rest
of the poem, louder.

Short Late October Pastoral

The lake is an overcast sky.
Three crows fly higher than I have ever seen crows fly.

The *Posted No Trespassing* sign hangs upside down.
The leaves pay no attention it.

Dream

I was not an old man.
She said, "I love you."
She said, "I'll wear my wedding dress."
I said, "No, don't. I'm married."
That was the only part of my dream that was not a dream.

First Day with Feeder

The flicker is the first
to find them as every
season. Then come the
crested titmice, and
the blue jays arrive,
only the two, and their
crimson counterparts,
the cardinals, likewise
a pair, and thus another
year is come and gone.

The Library

School is out early,
now they congregate,
outside in the sun,
one has a basketball,
two or three on bikes,
they talk, who knows
what they are saying,
it is a language largely
unknown to me, or
inside by the bathrooms,
hair is the principle
issue, a few even take
out books, the studious
ones, their glasses give
them away, I wish them
all well, yes, but it is
these, the serious ones
that I tremble the most for.

Zhao Li Pauses

by the stump of an old oak tree.
He remembers it when it was
the home to a family of owls.
He remembers pausing there
to listen to the cries of the owlets.
"Where are you now, you baby
owls I paused to listen to?"
Zhao Li wonders. "We have flown,
we have flown like the years
of your life, Zhao Li," he hears
them say from far, far away.

Three Deer

They belong here,
these three deer
grazing on my lawn.
They fit so much
better than we
having, unlike us, cut
no tree, upturned
no stone, cleared no
land as we do to force
ourselves onto
this space. No, no,
all they had to do
was to get here,
where they belong.

Zhao Li Finishes the Poem He Began 70 Years Ago

When I was 8 years old,
they told me I looked
like my mother. When
I was 28 years old, they
told me I looked like my
father. When I was 48
years old, they told me
I looked like my aunt.
When I was 68 years old,
they told me I looked like
my uncle. Now I am 78
years old. I look like myself.

Dreams

When I awaken from sleep,
and, clear-eyed, I see my dream
for what it is, for who dreams it,
how can I not know that it is
the same dream time and time
again since I myself am, time
and time again, the same dreamer
who falls into the same sleep to dream it?

Irony

It's not for me, not
anymore, not since out-
growing that wise guy's
plaything and letting
the convolutions, wrinkles,
creases of my mind go flat.

Shangri-La

It is always a valley,
except the Garden
of Eden, which was
an oasis in a desert,
which was a mirage,
which a valley can never be.

November Woods

The woods are empty
but for the sticks we
still must find ourselves
calling trees, the flesh
of their leaves half a foot
thick on the ground.

Two Dogs

A man walking two
dogs is not the same
as a woman walking
two dogs, especially
if they are the same
two dogs. Ask the dogs.
They know very well.

Youth

When I was younger,
Bill, it was plain to me
that, unlike you, I must
not "make something
of myself." I think I was
waiting for the world to
make something of me,
which, of course, it did
not although it could have,
had it really wanted to.
There is precedent
for such anomaly.

Prayer

O Goddess
of Euphoria,
Come O Dopa
mine of mine!

War

The war clears
to reveal the fog.

The fog clears
to reveal the smoke.

The smoke clears
to reveal the dead.

The dead clear
to reveal the future.

The future clears
to reveal the wars.

Empty Field in Which There Used to Be Three Horses

They are not a memory, for an
empty field cannot remember what
grazed on its grasses. What it remembers
is only that it can, for another year, grow
more grasses for grazing on or not.

Zhao Li Wanted to Know

when he got to be so old,
so he went out and stood
next to the wise old wild
black cherry tree. "Tell me,
wise old man, do you know
when I got to be so old?"
he asked. "Yes, I do, Zhao
Li. You were standing right
here next to me the whole
time," said the wise old
wild black cherry tree.

Songbird in the Snow

It snowed during the night.
I am drawn to the window
to listen to a songbird
singing on a branch of a tree
covered in snow. I listen.
I think it is singing the same
song it sang in the spring.
I listen. It does not sound
the same. Something about
it is different. Perhaps it is
the way all the snow absorbs
the song, or perhaps it is the way
the songbird has talked itself
into singing in all the snow.

Snow

It snowed during the night.
It is a wet snow.
It is a heavy snow.
It is a depressing snow.
It is a snow that presses down
its first small cold representation
of oppression onto the unsuspecting world.

The Consolations

We must be consoled.
We must console ourselves.
Every day we need consolation,
for we would not be human if we did not.
Some of us know the consolation of religion.
Some of us the consolation of philosophy.
Some of us the consolation of music.
Some of us the consolation of art.
Some of us the consolation of drink.
Some of us must know more than one to be consoled properly.
I know the consolations of music, of wine, and of poetry.
I know the consolation of the warm embrace of the music of the
    wine of poetry.

About the Author

Nominated for the National Book Award, the Eric Hoffer Book Award, and nominated three times for the Pulitzer Prize, J.R. Solonche is the author of more than 40 books of poetry and coauthor of another. He lives in the Hudson Valley.

www.ingramcontent.com/pod-product-compliance
Lightning Source LLC
Chambersburg PA
CBHW022016160426
43197CB00007B/453